A PRACTICAL AND SIMPLE GUIDE
TO A HOME MORTGAGE

by Gary J. Bass

G&P PUBLISHING

Library of Congress Catalog Card Number 87-82025
International Standard Book Number 0-944319-00-9

G&P Publishing
P.O. Box 157096
Irving, Texas 75015-7096

Printed in the United States of America
Cover design by Enhanced Image

DEDICATION

To all of the Mortgage
Loan Professionals,
who shared their knowledge
with me,
as Co-workers and Friends.
To Pat and Joe.
To my wife, Paula, for Believing.

TABLE OF CONTENTS

Page

PREFACE

This book was written as a *simple* guide for those people interested in buying their first house, or their next house. The book will guide you through the home buying process. You will learn how to determine what price house you can qualify to buy based on your income and expenses. I also give you suggestions on finding a house, selecting a mortgage lender, preparing for your mortgage application and how to follow the entire mortgage process. All of the math is shown in simple step-by-step examples.

Above all, I have made the process simple to follow and understand. I give you information that can save you money and educate you about the home buying process. There are sample worksheets to guide you and a glossary that defines 'mortgage talk'.

This is not intended as a scholarly work on the mortgage business. I have included only those items that I feel will be useful to you in obtaining a home mortgage. Simplicity is my upmost desire in providing this material. I am confident you will find this book to be a valuable tool in obtaining a home beneficial to you, your nerves and your bank account.

Gary J. Bass

CHAPTER ONE

How To Qualify for A Loan
Underwriting Ratios
Conventional,
FHA & VA Loans

You may want to purchase your first house, your next house, or refinance your present home. For either, the home buying process can be a puzzling, mysterious experience. Having gone through the procedure once does not make one an expert, because you have probably forgotten the questions asked, information needed, required qualifications and the rest of the involved process. Speaking of refinancing, some people try to refinance their homes only to find out they do not qualify for a new, lower payment, with a lower interest rate than they presently hold. And this is the home they are presently living in and making monthly payments to a lender. Qualifying is important.

Most people want to know first if they are elegible to buy a home, and if so, what price house. Mortgage lenders use 'underwriting ratios' to qualify potential borrowers. Underwriting ratios are stated as 28/36, 25/33, 33/38 or similar ratios for most conventional loans. Conventional loans are loans other than FHA or VA loans.

The first number in the 'underwriting ratio', called the 'front-end' ratio, represents the percentage of your gross monthly income you will be allowed to spend on your monthly house payment. The second number, called the 'back-end' ratio, represents the percentage of your gross monthly income you will be allowed to spend on your projected montly house payment plus all of your monthly bills.

1

I will give you an example. Let's say a family has a gross annual income of $35,000. Divide $35,000 by 12 for the gross monthly income of $2,916.67, or $2,917.00 rounded off. We will use 28/36 as our underwriting ratio. Take 28% of $2,917.00 and you get $816.76 ($2,917 x .28 = $816.76). This means you will be allowed to spend $816.76 for your total monthly house payment. This figure represents the principal payment (repaying the borrowed amount), plus interest payment, insurance, taxes and, perhaps, mortgage insurance (these will be discussed later).

Now, we will take the 'back-end' ratio. Since we are using 28/36 as the underwriting ratio, we will take 36% of the gross monthly income of $2,917.00, which equals $1,050.12 ($2,917 x .36 = $1,050.12). This means that this family would be allowed to spend $1,050.12 each month on their projected monthly house payment *plus* their regular monthly bills. The projected monthly house payment is $816.76 so that would leave $233.36 for monthly bills ($1,050.12 less $816.76 = $233.36).

Sometimes, bills that will be paid off in ten months, or less, paying the *minimum* monthly payment, will not be included in the back ratio. However, I would include all bills so you will have a 'worst case' example. By this, I mean you will be able to tell what your total monthly bills are that may have to be included in the underwriting ratios.

Basically, the underwriting ratios used depend on the amount of the down payment. With a 5% down payment (a 95% loan), the underwriting ratios will be more strict than on a loan with a 10% down payment (a 90% loan). Underwriting ratios of 25/33 may be used on a 95% loan and ratios of 28/36 may be used on a 90% loan. In some cases, with a 25%, or larger, down payment, the underwriting ratios may be as high as 33/38. The more money a borrower puts down, the safer a lender feels in loaning money for a house.

To figure a down payment, divide the amount of money used for a down payment by the sales price of a house. For example, if $10,000 is the down payment and $90,000 is the sales price, divide $10,000 by $90,000 and the answer is 11, or 11%. This means the down payment is 11% of the sales price, or an 89% loan. Lenders call this the 'loan-to-value-ratio' (LTVR). The LTVR for this example would be 89% (100% minus 11% = 89%).

Lenders standardize loan-to-value-ratios into several loan amounts. Generally, these are 95% loans, 90%, 85% and 80% and below. If a LTVR falls between these ratios, the loan is usually considered to be at the higher ratio. For example, the 89% loan above would be considered a 90% loan. A 93% LTVR would be considered a 95% loan. This is for the purpose of determining the proper underwriting ratio. Some lenders do not use 85% but go directly from 90% to 80%. In this case, a 83% loan may be considered a 90% loan, depending on the lender.

The underwriting ratios I have used so far apply only to conventional loans. I will discuss FHA and VA loans later in this chapter. The following information applies to all types of loans.

The largest part of your house payment will be the principal and interest payment. To figure your principal and interest payment, determine the loan amount you would need to borrow from a lender. Using the previous example, a $10,000 down payment, on a sales price of $90,000, would leave a loan amount of $80,000 ($90,000 minus $10,000 = $80,000).

Next, determine the number of thousands in the loan amount. A loan amount of $80,000 would have 80 thousands ($80,500 would have 80.5 thousands and $80,367 would have 80.367 thousands). Now turn to the last page in this chapter, titled 'Payment Factors', and we will find the factor that will determine the principal and interest payment.

Start in the upper left hand column titled 'Term Rate'. This column lists interest rates from 4% (shown as 4.000%) to 10.5% and continues on the right hand side of the page from 10.625% to 17%. The columns to the right of the 'Term Rate' columns represent the amount of time (in years) loans are paid out. Though the pay-out times listed are 30, 25, 20 and 15 years, most loans fall into either the 30 or 15 year range. The longer the term, the lower the monthly payment (and more total interest paid.

Look at the 'Payment Factors' chart and I will explain the rates. Look at the second number shown in the left hand 'Term Rate' column. The number is 4.125. The first digit, 4, represents a whole number. The .125 represents a decimal, or a fraction. .125 is the same as 1/8th. So, 4.125 equals 4 and one-eighth percent. Sometimes interest rates will be given as a fraction and sometimes as a decimal. The following chart will enable you to change from fractions to decimals and the reverse, from decimals to fractions.

FRACTIONS		DECIMALS
1/8th	=	.125
1/4th	=	.250
3/8th	=	.375
1/2	=	.500
5/8th	=	.625
3/4th	=	.750
7/8th	=	.875

To figure a principal and interest payment, we will need to have an interest rate, length of the desired pay-out and the number of thousands in the loan amount. Let us assume an interest rate of 10% for a period of 30 years (30) and a loan amount of $80,000, or 80 thousands.

Look on the PAYMENT FACTOR chart, at the end of this chapter, and find 10% (10.000) in the Term Rate column, on the bottom left hand side of the chart. When you locate this, go to the next column to the right, under "30 Yrs". The factor you will find is 8.78. Multiply the factor, 8.78 by the number of thousands in the loan amount, 80, and the answer is $702.40 (8.78 x 80 = $702.40). This represents the principal and interest payment. Add to this the taxes and insurance, and possibly the mortgage insurance payment, and you will have the total projected monthly house payment. (Note: The PAYMENT FACTORS shown on the chart at the end of this chapter are rounded off so the principal and interest payment obtained using these factors will not be exact but will be extremely close to the actual payment.)

To *approximate* what the actual monthly payment would be with the insurance, taxes and mortgage insurance added in, add 14% to the principal and interest amount. Using the above principal and interest amount of $702.40, multiply this amount by 14% and add that amount to $702.40 ($702.40 x .14 = $98.34. Use a shorter method by multiplying $702.40 by 1.14 and you get the same answer but skip one step.) Add the $98.34 to $702.40 and you get a total of $800.74. This is only an approximation of the total monthly payment but it will be close to the actual amount.

To be more exact, call an insurance agent and ask the cost of homeowners insurance on a house selling for $90,000, or whatever the sales price is on the house you have in mind. Then call a realtor and ask for a good guess for yearly taxes in the area you are looking. Or call your city and county taxing authority with the same question. Divide the taxes and insurance amounts by 12 to get the monthly amount.

Add these figures to the principal and interest amount and you should have an amount similar to what we figured above using 14%.

The Mortgage Insurance referred to above is a charge

the borrower will normally pay, if the loan-to-value-ratio is above 80%. This is insurance that protects the lender in case they have to take a loss due to a borrower's default. Since this reduces the lender's risk, they can offer lower interest rates. Generally, if the loan-to-value-ratio is 80%, or lower, mortgage insurance is normally not required. Again, the more money a borrower invests in a property, by a down payment, the better the lender feels about the loan.

Having arrived at a projected house payment, we are now ready to see if we qualify for a loan by using the underwriting ratios. We will assume a borrower has a gross annual income of $35,000, with a gross monthly income of $2,916.67, and is interested in a 30 year loan. We will also use an interest rate of 10% (10.000 on the PAYMENT FACTORS chart). Using the previous example, we know the principal and interest payment will be approximately $702.40 and the insurance, taxes and mortgage insurance will be approximately $98.34, for a total projected monthly house payment of $800.74. We will also assume the sales price of a house to be $90,000 and we are making a down payment of $9,000.00 (10% down) making a loan-to-value-ratio of 90%. (See Worksheet II at the end of this chapter. Using underwriting ratios of 28/36 for a 90% LTVR, divide the projected monthly house payment of $800.74 by the gross monthly income of $2,916.67 ($800.74 divided by $2,916.67 = .2745, or 27.5% rounded off). Since 27.5% is not over the 28% underwriting ratio, the 'front-end' ratio is all right for qualification.

To check the 'back-end' ratio, we will assume the borrower(s) pays monthly bills of $235.00. Add the $235.00 to the projected house payment of $800.74 for total projected monthly obligations of $1,035.74. Divide total obligations by the gross monthly income to check the 'back-end' ratio ($1,035.74 divided by $2,916.67 = .355, or 36% rounded off). Since the back-end ratio is not over

6

the allowable 36%, the ratio is all right.

If the underwriting ratios had been over the allowable limits, the borrowers would have to look for a lower priced house or check to make sure all monthly income had been included in the gross monthly income figure. Understand also that all sources of your income will have to be verified by the lender.

Another way to quickly determine the price house you will be able to afford is to do the following. This method is not exact but it will give you a close approximation. See Worksheet I at the end of this chapter. Take your gross monthly income, assume $2,916.67, and multiply that by 28%, for an answer of $816.67 ($2,916.67 x .28 = $816.67). Multiply that answer, $816.67, by 14% ($816.67 x .14 = $114.33). The $114.33 represents the approximate amount of taxes, insurance and mortgage insurance added to the total monthly house payment.

Subtract the $114.33 from the total projected house payment of $816.67 and that leaves $702.34, which represents the approximate principal and interest payment. Using the same payment factor for 10% (10.000), 8.78, divide the $702.34 by 8.78 for an answer of 79.99. This answer, representing the maximum loan amount, is presented in thousands so add three zeros (000) for a total of $79,990.00. Add to this figure the projected amount you intend to place as a down payment and you have a price of $89,990.00. This tells you the approximate sales price you can afford, approximately $90,000.

FHA

The Federal Housing Administration (FHA) insures its loans and allows a lower down payment, in most instances, than a conventional loan. The minimum down payment is usually around five (5) percent.

The FHA sets maximum loan amounts that vary across

the country. Presently, $90,000 is the maximum loan amount but check with mortgage lenders, or realtors, in your area to determine the maximum loan amount for your town or city.

The main difference between FHA and conventional underwriting ratios is that FHA uses a 'net' monthly income figure as opposed to 'gross' monthly income for conventional loans. See Worksheet III at the end of this chapter and we will go over the FHA qualifying process.

To obtain your 'net' monthly income, subtract the monthly income tax that is deducted from your monthly paycheck. That is your net income. Next, you need to figure the principal and interest payment just as we figured it in the preceding examples. We will use the previous example here. The principal and interest payment was $702.40 and the total figure, including taxes and insurance, was $800.74. FHA also figures a monthly 'Maintenance and Repair' amount and an average monthly 'Utility' expense. Both of these amounts are determined by the square footage of the house. The amounts vary across the country so call a local lender for local figures, giving the lender the square footage of the house.

The next step is to add all of your monthly expenses, including bills, social security, child support and child care. We can now figure front-end and back-end ratios just as before. The underwriting ratios used by FHA are 38/53.

To obtain the front-end ration, divide the total monthly payment (assume $1,050.00 with the added maintenance and utility expense) by the net monthly income figure (assume a net income of $2,463.67, which is the previous gross monthly income we used but deducting income tax for a family of three). Divide $1,050.00 by $2,463.67 and you get .426, or .43 rounded off (43%). Since 38% is the maximum ratio, the borrower would not qualify using these ratios.

However, the borrower may be able to qualify using

the 'Residual Income' formula. Taking the same projected monthly house payment, you subtract social security, monthly bills, child support and child care expense from the net monthly income figure. You then compare that remainder with the FHA 'Residual Income Chart' shown on the bottom of Worksheet III. By looking at the chart, you can see that a family of three would have to have $781.00 left over after everything was subtracted from the net income. So, if a borrower does not qualify using FHA underwriting ratios, it may be possible to qualify using the Residual Formula.

VA

The Veterans Administration guarantees its loans and allows a veteran to purchase a home with little, or no, down payment. The qualifying method is similar to FHA qualifying.

Veterans, unremarried widows of veterans, or unremarried wives of veterans who are listed as missing in action (MIA) may be eligible for VA loans. You can check with the Veterans Administration, or mortgage lenders, to see if you qualify for veteran's benefits. I will list the paperwork and documentation you will need to take for a mortgage application in a later chapter.

Worksheet IV, at the end of this chapter, will guide you through the qualifying process. Assume the same principal and interest payment we used in both preceding problems, $702.40. Use the *gross* monthly income, $2,916.67, and subtract the monthly income tax, social security, retirement, monthly bills, child support payments, child care payments (see note on worksheet beside 'child care payments'), job related expense (see note beside this deduction) and the projected house payment. The house payment, for VA qualifying, consists of the principal and interest payment, taxes and insurance (figured at $2.00

9

per thousand, based on the loan amount). Compare the remaining amount with the residual income chart at the bottom of the worksheet. For a family of three, The residual income would need to be at least $781.00. Since, in the example, there was a monthly residual of $992.73, this example would qualify using residuals.

VA also uses a Ratio Formula, detailed on the worksheet. Basically, you take the total of the monthly bills, plus total house payment, with VA maintenance, Utilities and Air Conditioning and divide that total by the gross monthly income. The result cannot be over 41%. In this example, 43.3% was over the 41% maximum. Since the Residual qualifying was all right, VA would have to decide whether or not to approve this loan.

The Maximum loan amount VA allows, with no down payment, is $110,000. The maximum loan amount can go up to $135,000 with a down payment. Check with a mortgage lender, or real estate agent, for more specifics.

WORKSHEET I

DETERMINING MAXIMUM LOAN AMOUNT AND SALES PRICE

<u>EXAMPLE:</u>

What can I afford with a gross income of $35,000 per year?

$2,916.67	Gross monthly income
x .28	Multiplied by 28% front-end ratio
$ 816.67	Maximum allowable house payment
x .14	Multiply by 14% to approximate taxes and insurance
$ 114.33	
- - - - - -	Approximate taxes and insurance
$ 816.67	Maximum allowable house payment from above
− 144.33	
	Subtract approximate taxes and insurance
$ 702.34	Principal and interest payment
÷ 8.78	Divide by the payment factor for interest rate (10%) - See payment Factor page in this chapter
79.993166 = $79,993.17	<u>Maximum loan amount</u>
+10,000.00	Add projected down payment
$89,993.17	<u>Maximum sales price</u> (rounded off - $90,000)

<u>YOUR EXAMPLE:</u>

$	Gross monthly income
x	Multiplied by front-end ratio (25%, 28%, 33%)
$	Maximum allowable house payment
x	Multiply by 14% to approximate taxes and insurance
$	Approximate taxes and insurance
- - - - -	
$	Maximum allowable house payment from above
−	Subtract approximate taxes and insurance
$	Principal and interest payment
÷	Divide by the payment factor for interest rate
= $	Maximum loan amount
+	Add projected down payment
	Maximum sales price

11

WORKSHEET II

CONVENTIONAL LOAN QUALIFYING GUIDELINES

GROSS MONTHLY INCOME $\underline{\$2,916.67}$ (A)

PROPOSED MONTHLY MORTGAGE PAYMENT:

Principal and Interest	$702.40
Additional Monthly Costs	1.14
(Taxes, insurance, etc.)	$800.74

APPROXIMATE MONTHLY HOUSE PAYMENT $ 800.74 (B)

MONTHLY BILLS: $ 235.00 (C)

TOTAL OBLIGATIONS: (B+C) $1,051.82 (D)

FRONT-END RATIO:

$\dfrac{\$800.74}{\text{(B) Total Monthly Mortgage Payment}}$ divided by $\dfrac{\$2,916.67}{\text{(A) Gross Monthly Income}}$

equals $\dfrac{27.5\%}{\text{Front-end Ratio}}$ (must be 28% or less)*

BACK-END RATIO:

$\dfrac{\$1,051.82}{\text{(D) Total Obligations}}$ divided by $\dfrac{\$2,916.67}{\text{(A) Gross Monthly Income}}$

equals $\dfrac{36\%}{\text{Back-end Ratio}}$ (Must be 36% or less)*

See the next page for a blank Worksheet II.

*The underwriting ratios you use may be 28/36, 25/33, or even 33/38, depending on your Loan-to-Value-Ratio (LTVR). The ratio of 28/36 seems to be the most used.

WORKSHEET II

CONVENTIONAL LOAN QUALIFYING GUIDELINES

GROSS MONTHLY INCOME   \$_____ (A)

PROPOSED MONTHLY MORTGAGE PAYMENT:

     Principal and Interest   \$

     Additional Monthly Costs   x_____
     (taxes, insurance, etc)

     APPROXIMATE MONTHLY HOUSE PAYMENT   \$_____ (B)

MONTHLY BILLS: \$_____ (C)

TOTAL OBLICATIONS: (B+C)   \$_____ (D)

FRONT-END RATIO:

_____ divided by _____
(B) Total Monthly Mortgage Payment   (A) Gross Monthly Income

equals_____ (must be 28% or less)*
     Front-end Ratio

BACK-END RATIO:

_____
(D) Total Obligations   divided by   (A) Gross Monthly Income

equals_____ (must be 36% or less)*
     Back-end Ratio

*The underwriting ratios you use may be 28/36, 25/33, or even 33/38, depending on your Loan-to-Value-Ratio (LTVR). The ratio of 28/36 seems to be the most used.

WORKSHEET III

FHA QUALIFYING FORMULAS

RATIO FORMULA

GROSS MONTHLY INCOME: Borrower $_____ Co-Borrower $_____		$2,916.67
	LESS: Monthly Income Tax	− $ 453.00
	NET EFFECTIVE INCOME	= $2,463.67 (A)

ADD: HOUSING EXPENSE

Principal & Interest	$702.40	
Taxes	$_____	
Insurance	$_____	
Utilities	$_____	
Maintenance & Repair	$_____	
TOTAL HOUSING EXPENSE	$_____	$1,050.00 (B)

ADD: OTHER EXPENSES

SOCIAL SECURITY (7.15% of monthly
income to a maximum of $250.25 per
employed person. 12.3% to a maximum of
$430.50 per self-employed person.) $208.54 ($2,916.67 x .0715)

RETIREMENT (8.5% for Federal
employees. Teachers and city &
county workers deduct normal
contributions.) $_____

TOTAL MONTHLY BILLS	$235.00	
CHILD SUPPORT/ALIMONY	$_____	

CHILD CARE (Children under 10 years
of age. Need actual amount.) $_____

TOTAL OTHER EXPENSES	$ 443.54 (C)
TOTAL HOUSING AND OTHER EXPENSE (B+C)	$1,493.54 (D)

FRONT-END RATIO:

$$\frac{(B)\ \$1,050.00}{\text{Total Housing Expense}} \quad \text{divided by} \quad \frac{(A)\ \$2,463.67}{\text{Net Effective Income}} \quad = .426,\ \text{or } 42.6\%$$
(Maximum of 38%)

BACK-END RATIO:

$$\frac{(D)\ \$1,493.54}{\text{Housing + Other Expenses}} \quad \text{divided by} \quad \frac{(A)\ \$2,463.67}{\text{Net Effective Income}} \quad = .606,\ \text{or } 60.6\%$$
(Maximum of 53%)

(Borrower does not qualify by this method. Ratios too high.)

— — — — — — — — — — — — — —

RESIDUAL INCOME FORMULA

GROSS MONTHLY INCOME OF BORROWER & CO-BORROWER	$2,916.67
LESS: Income Tax	− $ 453.00
LESS: Social Security	− $ 208.54
LESS: Retirement	− $
LESS: Total Housing Expense (B)	− $1,050.00
LESS: Total Monthly Bills	− $ 235.00
LESS: Child Support/Alimony	− $
LESS: Child Care	− $
AMOUNT REMAINING FOR FAMILY SUPPORT	$ 970.13

RESIDUAL INCOME CHART*

One person...........................$409	Family of 5.........................$946
Two persons.........................$643	Family of 6.........................$1,021
Family of 3..........................$781	Family of 7.........................$1,096
Family of 4..........................868	Add $75 for each additional family member

(Borrowers qualify by residual income formula. A family of 3 needs a residual income of $781 and they
have $970.13) *Amounts vary by area. Check with a local lender or FHA.

14

WORKSHEET III

FHA QUALIFYING FORMULAS

RATIO FORMULA

GROSS MONTHLY INCOME: Borrower $_____ Co-Borrower $_____ $_____
                      LESS: Monthly Income Tax   − $_____
                            NET EFFECTIVE INCOME   = $_____ (A)

ADD: HOUSING EXPENSE
  Principal & Interest $_____
  Taxes $_____
  Insurance $_____
  Utilities $_____
  Maintenance & Repair $_____
  TOTAL HOUSING EXPENSE $_____ $_____ (B)

ADD: OTHER EXPENSES
  SOCIAL SECURITY (7.15% of monthly
  income to a maximum of $250.25 per
  employed person. 12.3% to a maximum of
  $430.50 per self-employed person.) $_____
  RETIREMENT (8.5% for Federal
  employees. Teachers and city &
  county workers deduct normal
  contributions.) $_____
  TOTAL MONTHLY BILLS $_____
  CHILD SUPPORT/ALIMONY $_____
  CHILD CARE (Children under 10 years
  of age. Need actual amount.) $_____
  TOTAL OTHER EXPENSES $_____ (C)
  TOTAL HOUSING AND OTHER EXPENSE (B+C) $_____ (D)

FRONT-END RATIO:

$$\frac{(B)}{\text{Total Housing Expense}} \text{ divided by } \frac{(A)}{\text{Net Effective Income}} = \underset{\text{(Maximum of 38\%)}}{\qquad}$$

BACK-END RATIO:

$$\frac{(D)}{\text{Housing + Other Expenses}} \text{ divided by } \frac{(A)}{\text{Net Effective Income}} = \underset{\text{(Maximum of 53\%)}}{\qquad}$$

(Borrower does not qualify by this method. Ratios too high.)

— — — — — — — — — — — — — —

RESIDUAL INCOME FORMULA

GROSS MONTHLY INCOME OF BORROWER & CO-BORROWER $_____
  LESS: Income Tax   − $_____
  LESS: Social Security   − $_____
  LESS: Retirement   − $_____
  LESS: Total Housing Expense (B)   − $_____
  LESS: Total Monthly Bills   − $_____
  LESS: Child Support/Alimony   − $_____
  LESS: Child Care   − $_____
AMOUNT REMAINING FOR FAMILY SUPPORT $_____

RESIDUAL INCOME CHART*

One person............................$409	Family of 5.........................$ 946
Two persons...........................$643	Family of 6.........................$1,021
Family of 3...........................$781	Family of 7.........................$1,096
Family of 4...........................$868	Add $75 for each additional family member

*Amounts vary by area. Check with a local lender or FHA.

15

WORKSHEET IV

VA QUALIFYING

GROSS MONTHLY INCOME OF VETERAN AND SPOUSE	$2,916.67 (A)
LESS: Monthly Income Tax	$ 453.00
LESS: Social Security (7.15% of monthly income to a	
to a maximum of $250.25 per employed person.	
12.3% to a maximum of $430.50 per	
self-employed person.)	$ 208.54
LESS: Retirement (8.5% for Federal employees.	
• Teachers and city & county workers	
deduct normal contributions.)	$
LESS: Total Monthly Bills	$ 235.00 (B)
LESS: Child Support/Alimony Payments	$ (C)
LESS: Child Care Payments (If spouse works and	
has children under age 10.)	$
LESS: Job Related Expense ($50 for couple with	
no children. OMIT if Child Care	
payments are deducted.)	$
LESS: Monthly House Payment	
Principal & Interest Payment	$ 702.40 (D)
Taxes & Insurance ($2.00 per thousand based	
on loan amount. EX. $80,000 = 80	
thousands; $80,500 = 80.5 thousands.)	$ 160.00 (E)
Maintenance & Utilities (See chart below -	
based on square footage of house and	
whether frame or brick.)	$ 130.00 (F)
Air Conditioning (See chart below)	$ 35.00 (G)
AMOUNT REMAINING FOR FAMILY SUPPORT -	
RESIDUAL FORMULA	$ 992.73

Compare above figure with Redidual Income Chart below

RATIO FORMULA

$ 1,262.40	divided by	$ 2,916.67	=	.433, or 43.3%
(B+C+C+D+E+F+G)		(A)		(Maximum of 41%

MAINTENANCE & UTILITIES			
Area (Sq. Ft.)	Frame	Brick	A/C
800	75	65	30
900	87	75	30
1000	100	87	30
1100	115	100	35
1200	130	115	35
1300	140	130	35
1400	147	135	45
1500	153	140	45
1600	160	147	45
1700	165	153	45
1800-2000	175	160	55
2000-2400	195	175	60
Over 2400	210	195	65

RESIDUAL INCOME CHART

One person..................$ 409
Veteran & Spouse.............$ 643
Family of 3..................$ 781
Family of 4..................$ 868
Family of 5..................$ 946
Family of 6..................$1,021
Family of 7..................$1,096
Add $75 for each additional family member.

16

WORKSHEET IV

VA QUALIFYING

GROSS MONTHLY INCOME OF VETERAN AND SPOUSE	$_____	(A)
LESS: Monthly Income Tax	$_____	
LESS: Social Security (7.15% of monthly income to a to a maximum of $250.25 per employed person. 12.3% to a maximum of $430.50 per self-employed person.)	$_____	
LESS: Retirement (8.5% for Federal employees. Teachers and city & county workers deduct normal contributions.)	$_____	
LESS: Total Monthly Bills	$_____	(B)
LESS: Child Support/Alimony Payments	$_____	(C)
LESS: Child Care Payments (If spouse works and has children under age 10.)	$_____	
LESS: Job Related Expense ($50 for couple with no children. OMIT if Child Care payments are deducted.)	$_____	
LESS: Monthly House Payment		
Principal & Interest Payment	$_____	(D)
Taxes & Insurance ($2.00 per thousand based on loan amount. EX. $80,000 = 80 thousands; $80,500 = 80.5 thousands.)	$_____	(E)
Maintenance & Utilities (See chart below - based on square footage of house and whether frame or brick.)	$_____	(F)
Air Conditioning (See chart below)	$_____	(G)

AMOUNT REMAINING FOR FAMILY SUPPORT -

RESIDUAL FORMULA $_____

Compare above figure with Redidual Income Chart below

RATIO FORMULA

$_____ divided by $_____ = _____

(B+C+C+D+E+F+G)   (A)   (Maximum of 41%)

MAINTENANCE & UTILITIES

Area (Sq. Ft.)	Frame	Brick	A/C
800	75	65	30
900	87	75	30
1000	100	87	30
1100	115	100	35
1200	130	115	35
1300	140	130	35
1400	147	135	45
1500	153	140	45
1600	160	147	45
1700	165	153	45
1800-2000	175	160	55
2000-2400	195	175	60
Over 2400	210	195	65

RESIDUAL INCOME CHART

One person.................$ 409
Veteran & Spouce............$ 643
Family of 3.................$ 781
Family of 4.................$ 868
Family of 5.................$ 946
Family of 6.................$1,021
Family of 7.................$1,096
Add $75 for each additional family member.

17

PAYMENT FACTORS
Principal And Interest Factors Per $1,000 Of Loan Amount

TERM RATE	30 Yrs.	25 Yrs.	20 Yrs.	15 Yrs.
4.000%	4.77	5.28	6.06	7.40
4.125	4.85	5.35	6.13	7.46
4.250	4.92	5.42	6.19	7.52
4.375	5.00	5.49	6.26	7.59
4.500	5.07	5.56	6.33	7.65
4.625	5.14	5.63	6.39	7.71
4.750	5.22	5.70	6.47	7.78
4.875	5.29	5.78	6.53	7.84
5.000	5.37	5.85	6.60	7.91
5.125	5.44	5.92	6.67	7.97
5.250	5.52	5.99	6.74	8.04
5.375	5.60	6.07	6.81	8.11
5.500	5.68	6.14	6.88	8.18
5.625	5.76	6.22	6.95	8.24
5.750	5.83	6.29	7.02	8.30
5.875	5.92	6.37	7.09	8.37
6.000	6.00	6.44	7.16	8.44
6.125	6.08	6.52	7.24	8.51
6.250	6.16	6.60	7.31	8.57
6.375	6.24	6.67	7.38	8.64
6.500	6.32	6.75	7.46	8.71
6.625	6.40	6.83	7.53	8.78
6.750	6.49	6.91	7.60	8.85
6.875	6.57	6.99	7.68	8.92
7.000	6.65	7.07	7.75	8.99
7.125	6.74	7.15	7.83	9.06
7.250	6.82	7.23	7.90	9.13
7.375	6.91	7.31	7.98	9.20
7.500	6.99	7.39	8.06	9.27
7.625	7.08	7.47	8.13	9.34
7.750	7.16	7.55	8.21	9.41
7.875	7.25	7.64	8.29	9.48
8.000	7.34	7.72	8.36	9.56
8.125	7.42	7.80	8.44	9.63
8.250	7.51	7.88	8.52	9.70
8.375	7.60	7.97	8.60	9.77
8.500	7.69	8.05	8.68	9.85
8.625	7.78	8.14	8.76	9.92
8.750	7.87	8.22	8.84	9.99
8.875	7.96	8.31	8.92	10.07
9.000	8.05	8.39	9.00	10.14
9.125	8.14	8.48	9.08	10.22
9.250	8.23	8.56	9.16	10.29
9.375	8.32	8.65	9.24	10.37
9.500	8.41	8.74	9.32	10.44
9.625	8.50	8.82	9.40	10.52
9.750	8.59	8.91	9.49	10.59
9.875	8.68	9.00	9.57	10.67
10.000	8.78	9.09	9.65	10.75
10.125	8.87	9.18	9.73	10.82
10.250	8.96	9.26	9.81	10.90
10.375	9.05	9.35	9.90	10.98
10.500	9.15	9.44	9.98	11.05

TERM RATE	30 Yrs.	25 Yrs.	20 Yrs.	15 Yrs.
10.625%	9.24	9.53	10.07	11.13
10.750	9.33	9.62	10.15	11.18
10.875	9.43	9.71	10.24	11.29
11.000	9.52	9.80	10.32	11.37
11.125	9.62	9.89	10.41	11.44
11.250	9.71	9.98	10.49	11.52
11.375	9.81	10.07	10.58	11.60
11.500	9.90	10.16	10.66	11.68
11.625	10.00	10.26	10.75	11.76
11.750	10.09	10.35	10.84	11.84
11.875	10.19	10.44	10.92	11.92
12.000	10.29	10.53	11.01	12.00
12.125	10.38	10.62	11.10	12.08
12.250	10.48	10.72	11.19	12.16
12.375	10.58	10.81	11.27	12.24
12.500	10.67	10.90	11.36	12.33
12.625	10.77	11.00	11.45	12.41
12.750	10.87	11.09	11.54	12.49
12.875	10.96	11.18	11.63	12.57
13.000	11.06	11.28	11.72	12.65
13.125	11.16	11.37	11.80	12.73
13.250	11.26	11.47	11.89	12.82
13.375	11.36	11.56	11.98	12.90
13.500	11.45	11.66	12.07	12.98
13.625	11.55	11.75	12.16	13.07
13.750	11.65	11.85	12.25	13.15
13.875	11.75	11.94	12.34	13.23
14.000	11.85	12.04	12.44	13.32
14.125	11.95	12.13	12.53	13.40
14.250	12.05	12.23	12.62	13.49
14.375	12.15	12.33	12.71	13.57
14.500	12.25	12.42	12.80	13.66
14.625	12.35	12.52	12.89	13.74
14.750	12.44	12.61	12.98	13.83
14.875	12.54	12.71	13.08	13.91
15.000	12.64	12.81	13.17	14.00
15.125	12.74	12.91	13.26	14.08
15.250	12.84	13.00	13.35	14.17
15.375	12.94	13.10	13.45	14.25
15.500	13.05	13.20	13.54	14.35
15.625	13.15	13.30	13.63	14.43
15.750	13.25	13.39	13.73	14.51
15.875	13.35	13.49	13.82	14.60
16.000	13.45	13.59	13.91	14.69
16.125	13.55	13.69	14.01	14.77
16.250	13.65	13.79	14.10	14.86
16.375	13.75	13.88	14.19	14.95
16.500	13.85	13.98	14.29	15.04
16.625	13.95	14.08	14.38	15.13
16.750	14.05	14.18	14.48	15.21
16.875	14.16	14.28	14.57	15.30
17.00	14.26	14.38	14.67	15.39

CHAPTER TWO

Realtors and
'For Sale by Owner'

People looking for a new home usually start looking before knowing how much they can afford to spend on a house. An experienced, knowledgable realtor can be a big help. Most realtors know how to qualify prospective buyers and usually do it well.

By knowing how to determine the price home for which you can qualify, you can save yourself, and a realtor, some valuable time. I recommend that most buyers should use a realtor. An experienced, knowledgable realtor can help smooth the entire process. How does one find an experienced, knowledgable realtor? Referrals are sometimes the best place to start. If you do not have any referrals, call a real estate office and talk with the owner or manager. Tell them you are looking for a realtor who is experienced at qualifying prospective home buyers and one who is knowledgable about current rates and local lenders. Remember, the person selling a house is the one paying the realtor's commission, not you.

However, you can find some good buys on homes that are being sold by owners. Sometimes a seller will reduce the sales price of a house by the amount of a realtor's commission, usually around 6%. Then again, sometimes the seller will ask for a market-competitive sales price.

In that situation, you have to be able to determine whether or not the price being offered is a good value. This is another reason I recommend a realtor. If you want to buy directly from an owner, there are books in the library to help you. A certified appraiser will compare a prospective house with similar homes by doing an appraisal. However, an appraiser costs money. You will have to have an appraisal on the home you decide to buy but you do not want to have every home appraised that seems a possibility. Here again, a realtor can show you several houses that will allow you to compare features and prices. A realtor can usually quickly tell you whether or not a sales price is high, low or comparable to similar houses.

Without a realtor, a buyer will have to determine whether or not the sales price is good, will have to negotiate a sales contract and locate and deal with a mortgage lender. By asking the right questions at each stage, a buyer can successfully do all of this. But, a realtor can be a real help and a good source of advice and information.

If you decide to use a realtor, interview several and select the one you feel has the most to offer. you do not have to use the first realtor you speak with. The decision is yours so find one with whom you feel you can work.

I am not being paid by realtors to recommend them. My experience in the mortgage business has shown me the benefits an experienced and knowledgable realtor can provide during the home buying process.

If you find a home you like and are unsure about whether or not you qualify, you can usually contact a mortgage company and ask them to qualify you. Because of time constraints, they cannot always do so but most will at least take the information and call you back. Give them your gross monthly income, approximate amount of your monthly bills and the loan amount and sales price of the house you are thinking about buying.

Chapter I also provides the information for you to be able to determine these answers for yourself.

CHAPTER THREE

Interest Rates
Points — Rate Lock-In
Floating Interest Rates

Once you have found a home that you feel is right for you, you need to know about interest rates, points and how to select a mortgage lender. If you have used a realtor, he or she should be able to recommend one or more mortgage companies. The realtor should have had experience with different companies and will usually have an opinion about which ones provide the best service. The realtor will be able to advise you about current interest rates and points in the market place. They can help guide you to good companies that provide good service.

Should you have a signed sales contract on a house and are ready to proceed, you need to determine what rates and points are being offered by lenders. Decide what payout term you desire, usually 30 or 15 years, and the loan amount.

Look up mortgage companies in the yellow pages of your phone book, or call the companies your realtor recommended. When you call, tell the lender you want rate quotes. Give them the sales price, loan amount, and payout term.

The information you will receive will usually be in the following order; interest rate, discount points and origination fee. It will look like this - 10% 2½ + 1. They might also include 'plus MI' (mortgage insurance). The last number, the origination fee, will usually be 1 consistently, regardless of the company.

One discount point is equal to 1% of the loan amount. If your loan amount is $90,000, one discount point equals

$900.00 ($90,000 x .01 = $900.00). For the above example, a $90,000 loan at 10% would cost you 3½ points (2½ + 1) for a total of $3,150.00 ($90,000 x .035 = $3,150.00).

The discount points can go higher or lower depending on the interest rate. For instance, using the same example of 10% 2½ + 1, the mortgage company could probably offer a rate of 9 7/8% 3 + 1 or 10 1/8% 2 + 1. As the interest rate goes higher, points usually go lower. When interest rates go lower, points usually go higher.

The above rate quotes are basically the same. If you want to pay a larger amount at closing, for a lower interest rate, you can. However, if money is tight, you might take a higher interest rate in order to lower the discount points and thus decrease the closing cost.

If you make a down payment of less than 20% of the sales price, Mortgage Insurance will probably be required by lenders. This, again, is insurance that protects the lender against losses that may be incurred due to default or foreclosure. This will add from 1 to 2% at closing, plus a small monthly payment. Assuming 1% is added to our example for MI, that would increase the total points to 4½%, including the origination fee. The less the down payment, the higher the mortgage insurance. The higher the down payment, the lower the mortgage insurance cost. Generally, if a buyer puts a large down payment on a house, the safer the loan is from default. People are a lot less likely to walk away from a house they have $10,000 invested in than a house with $5,000 invested.

Mortgage companies package groups of loans together to sell to investors. The money the mortgage companies receive from investors goes into making money available for new loans. The interest rate, plus discount points, determine the worth of the loans, from an investor's view point.

An investor has to have a good return for the money invested in a loan package. If interest rates are low, higher discount points can make an investment worth while. On the other hand, if interest rates are higher, less discount points are necessary since the interest rate is high enough to provide a good investment.

The one percent origination fee goes to the lender to cover costs. The one percent, however, does not normally cover all costs. The mortgage companies frequently sell their loans to investors and retain 'servicing' on the loans. Servicing involves collecting payments, late charges, doing necessary paperwork and handling foreclosures and other problems. For this the lender is paid a fee by the investor.

Now, back to the interest rates. Interest rates and points are subject to change daily. When you call the different mortgage companies, ask them when their rates normally change during the day. Some companies change their rates in the morning, some in the afternoon. If you have received some rates that are somewhat higher, or lower, than most, this might be the reason. Several companies may have changed early in the day and others will change later in the day.

Make a list of companies you call. Include phone number, rate quotes and when, during the day, their rates are subject to change. It is usually a good idea to get the name of the person you spoke with so you can ask for that person the next time you call. You also need to ask whether or not they will lock in a rate and for how long.

Most companies, under normal market conditions, will lock-in interest rates and discount points for a period of time. During this time, the lender guarantees you the rate and points will not change. The length of a lock in varies between companies. Some companies will lock in rates for 30 days, some 45 and some 60 days. Processing a loan application, obtaining loan approval and preparing closing papers and closing and funding a loan can be done in thirty days but not often. Try to get an interest rate lock-in longer than 30 days, if you want to lock in a rate.

Sometimes, if you believe interest rates may go lower, you might decide to 'float' your rate. This means that you do not lock-in an interest rate but allow it to float. The floating rate will fluctuate with the market, sometimes being higher or lower than the original, or remaining the same. Some companies will allow you to lock in almost anytime while your loan is being processed and approved. With some companies, you will have to wait until approval is received to lock-in a rate and points.

If, after floating for a while, you choose to lock-in a rate, some companies will consider the loan application date as the first day of any guaranteed lock-in period. For example, assume you applied for a loan on May 1st and did not lock in a rate until May 15th. If the company has a 45 day lock-in, they may consider 15 days of your lock-in to have passed and you would have 30 days of lock-in remaining.

The lender takes all of the risk by locking in a rate. If interest rates go higher, the lender could get stuck with loans that will not sell because of the low interest rate. Lenders only offer a rate lock-in as an inducement to do business with them. However, sometimes an interest rate is locked in and rates go lower so that when the loan is ready to close, the market rates are lower than what the borrower locked-in. Normally, the borrower can negotiate with the lender for a lower rate.

If rates are lower that what you locked in, lenders will probably say that you would expect them to give you the rate you had locked in if interest rates had gone higher. If you switch to another company, you will have to duplicate some costs and wait for the other company to reprocess your loan. As stated above, you can usually negotiate a lower rate with your lender that will be satisfactory to both you and the company. If a lender says you can lock in an interest rate and points, be sure to *GET IT IN WRITING.*

If you float your rate the entire time, after approval, you should be allowed to lock-in your rate for a long enough period to allow you to close your loan and have the loan fund, normally 7 to 10 days.

In summary, when you contact lenders, make a list with the following information:

1. Name of lender, phone number and name of person with whom you spoke. Current interest rates, discount points and origination fee for the repayment period you chose, normally 30 or 15 years or a one year adjustable mortgage. Again, this will usually be given to you in figures like 10%, 2 + 1 (Plus MI).

2. Ask when rate changes are made during the day and note this.

3. Ask if interest rates and points can be locked in and for what length of time.

4. Ask them if you can float your rate and, if so, when you are allowed to lock-in a rate. Also, ask them when your lock-in period will begin. Will it be good from the application date or the date you lock in?

5. If you are considering floating a rate until approval, ask how long the lock-in period is after approval.

NOTE: For reasons I will discuss in the chapter on processing, your loan will have to be closed, funded and shipped to investors within ninety (90) days of the application date. Otherwise, various paperwork has to be updated. So try to close your loan as soon as possible.

CHAPTER FOUR

Fixed Rate and
Adjustable Rate Mortgages

This will not be an involved discussion of whether or not you should get a 15 year, 30 year or 1 year adjustable rate mortgage. I will list a few considerations for you to think about. Every family, or person, has different circumstances and considerations so there is not just one solution for everyone.

A Fixed Rate Mortgage is one that is paid off (amortized) in a given period of time, usually 15 or 30 years. With a fixed rate mortgage, the monthly payment remains the same for the full term. Using 15 years and 30 years as an example, the monthly payment is lower on a 30 year loan. However, the interest paid on a 30 year loan is almost double the interest of a 15 year loan.

If you intend to live in a house for 15 years and if you can qualify for a 15 year mortgage, then perhaps a 15 year loan is right for you. On the other hand, a lower 30 year payment might allow you to purchase furniture and appliances, if you need those. You might also intend to be in the house for a short time and look for appreciation to provide the equity you are looking for in your home, over a few years. There are many considerations and possibilities to go over. Talk with your realtor, financial adviser, a banker and your mortgage loan officer for other suggestions and advice.

Be sure and ask the mortgage lender if the loan you are considering has a prepayment penalty. If it does, you may decide to pay off your 30 year loan in 10, 15 or 20 years and discover you owe a fee for paying off the loan earlier than 30 years. There are not many of these loans around today but check and make sure.

The benefits of a fixed rate loan are that you know exactly what your payment is every month, allowing for easy budgeting, and the monthly payment should become easier and easier to handle with regular raises in your income.

If interest rates are low and you believe they will stay low for a few years, maybe an adjustable rate mortgage is for you. Though it is hard to pass up a low interest, fixed rate loan, there may be times when an adjustable rate mortgage (ARM) can be beneficial.

Should you transfer to an area and know you will only be there a short time, you may be interested in this type mortgage. Since rates for an ARM are normally lower than fixed rate mortgages, you can qualify for more house, or have lower payments than with a fixed rate. But examine this closely.

An adjustable rate mortgage is usually a 1 or 3 year adjustable. A one year adjustable is subject to a rate change every year and a three year adjustable every three years. Most adjustable mortgages have 'rate caps'. The caps limit the allowable increase for each adjustment period. If there is a yearly rate cap of 2, then the original rate can usually increase or decrease no more than 2% per year. For example, if a loan had an original interest rate of 10%, with yearly rate caps of 2%, the new rate could not be adjusted more than 2%. The new rate could not be lower than 8% nor more than 12%.

The adjustment will be based on some financial index. Many times the increase will be tied in to one, or three year U.S. Treasury securities.

To determine a new rate, the mortgage company will take the current index rate and add it to a 'margin'. The margin is an amount set by the mortgage company on your loan. The margin is added to the index to establish a new rate. If the loan has rate caps, the new amount cannot exceed the rate cap limits.

In addition to yearly rate caps, most ARMs have a lifetime maximum rate or a lifetime cap. A lifetime maximum rate is simply the maximum rate the loan allows. A lifetime cap establishes the maximum rate allowed by a cap rate. An adjustable rate mortgage might have a yearly rate cap of 2% and a lifetime cap of 5%. If the beginning rate was 7%, the maximum lifetime rate could never go above 12%.

Assume a borrower obtains an ARM with an initial interest rate of 7%, with a margin of 2.75% and a yearly rate cap of 2%. Since there is a yearly cap, the second year interest rate cannot go beyond 9%, with a lowest possible rate of 5%. Assume also that the index used is one year Treasury Securities.

To determine the new rate, at the end of the first year, take the current interest rate, 7%, add the margin, 2.75%, to the index, assume 5.81%, for a new rate of 8.56% (2.75% + 5.81% = 8.56%). This rate is normally rounded up to the nearest 1/8% so the new rate would be 8.625 (8 5/8%). The new rate is within the 2% yearly rate cap so it will apply. Had the new total been 9.56%, the yearly rate cap would have limited the new rate to 9%.

Mortgage lenders can give you all of the needed information for adjustable rate mortgages. You need to know the current rates, discount points and origination fee. Plus, the yearly rate cap, maximum rate allowed or lifetime rate cap (whichever applies), the margin and the index on which the adjustment is based. They should also be able to tell you what the index is currently and have a recent history of the index for the last few years, or months. Also, ask the lender whether or not their adjustable rate mortgage can be converted to a fixed rate mortgage and, if so, when it is allowed and what charges are involved.

Most people want, and have, fixed rate mortgages. Adjustable rate mortgages were designed during a time of high interest rates and allowed many people to buy a house when they would not have qualified under fixed rate guidelines.

Some adjustable rate mortgages have proven to be beneficial, others not so. Some ARMs allowed for negative amortization. To amortize a loan means to reduce the loan prinicipal by regular payments. Negative amortization means that the opposite occurs. Instead of reducing the original amount, the original amount increases.

The purpose of this type loan was to allow people to buy homes during periods of high interest rates, by offering low payments the first few years. Sometimes the low payments were not sufficient to amortize the loan so the difference between what was paid against what was needed was added back into the total loan amount. Some people ended up, a few years later, owing more for their home than the original loan amount.

Enough said about that. Just be sure to ask the lender if their adjustable rate mortgages have the possibility for negative amortization. Thank goodness very few loans today have this feature.

You will probably obtain a fixed rate mortgage. If you should have special circumstances that you feel warrant an adjustable rate mortgage, talk with a financial adviser and your loan officer and/or realtor.

There are also other variations of fixed rate mortgages that you may want to examine. Early-ownership loans enable a buyer to pay off a loan in fewer years and graduated payments increase the payment each year until a fixed payment is reached, usually four to five years. Ask your loan officer about these plans if you are interested. However, fixed rate loans are the most popular and usually the most beneficial.

CHAPTER FIVE

Information Needed for
the Mortgage Application

To prepare for the mortgage loan application, you will need to gather information. The more complete your information, the quicker and easier your loan can be processed. Your application will probably be taken by a loan officer or loan processor. I cannot stress enough the importance of thoroughly preparing the needed information for your loan application.

PROPERTY INFORMATION

The lender will first need information about the proposed new house. Most of that information will be on the sales contract you signed with the seller. That information includes street address, city, county, state and zip code. The legal description should be on the contract. Ask the seller, or realtor the age of the house.

PERSONAL INFORMATION

The next information will be personal information about the borrower, and co-borrower, if applicable. Since you know your names, we will skip that. You will be asked your age and how many years you attended school. Have your present address, how long you have lived there and verifiable addresses for the two past years. If you lived in apartments, provide the name of the apartments and the address of the manager or landlord who can verify your residency. Wherever you have lived for the past two years, you have to provide names and addresses of someone who can verify that fact.

You will be asked your marital status and number and ages of dependents. Supply an employment history covering two years, with addresses. You will be asked how long you have been in your present line of work, or profession, and how long you have been employed on your present job.

Most mortgage companies do not like to see that people have recently changed professions or their line of work. If you have, tie in the necessity of your prior work experience to your present job.

You will also be asked for your present position, or title, the type business in which you presently work, your social security number, home and business phone numbers.

INCOME INFORMATION

You will be required to supply your total gross, annual salary. If you receive any kind of bonus, your company will be asked to verify that you have received a bonus in the past, the amount and the probability of the bonus continuing in the future. If that cannot be verified, you may not be able to use that as additional income. Sometimes it can be verified with previous income tax returns from the past two years.

Should you be in a newly created position, a letter from your boss, or the payroll manager, stating that bonuses for similar positions have been paid and will likely continue to be paid will usually suffice. The letter will need to include projected bonus amounts. This is usually easy to obtain from your employer.

If you are on commission, or if the words 'sales' or 'marketing' appear in your job title, you will probably be asked to provide copies of your last two years tax returns (complete returns). That is the best way to verify past commissions and any other extra income that does not come from an employer.

A car allowance cannot be included in monthly income because it will be assumed as being reimbursement for money you have spent on car expenses.

Dividend and interest income should be included in your gross income but, again, you should be able to show a one to two year history of receiving such. Copies of tax returns can be used for this.

If you own rental property, you can include any net rental income. You will be asked to provide signed leases verifying the rent amounts. To get your net rental income, take the gross rent on a propety and subtract your mortgage payment on the property, along with taxes and insurance. The lender will take this net figure and allow a vacancy factor of 20-25%. You will then be credited with about 75% of your net rental income. The mortgages you have on any rental properties will have to be verified so provide the lender's name, address and account number.

ASSETS

You will need to list all of your assets as follows:

1. The lender will have to verify the source of your down payment and where the funds are located.

2. If there is a cash deposit on the new house, have the name and address of the person, or company holding the deposit.

3. List all checking and savings accounts, CDs, money market accounts and any other accounts you have. Have the name and address for each bank, or depository, and the account number. Also know how each account is titled (how the names are listed) and the present balance.

4. Have all of your stocks and bonds listed with present market values. You will have to prove you have the stocks and bonds. The best way is

to show your most recent monthly statement, if the securities are held by a company for you, or take the certificates with you to the application. The lender will make copies for you. Also know the present value of the stocks and bonds.

5. If you have life insurance that contains cash value, have that amount. Your insurance agent can tell you the amount.

6. Real Estate Owned - You will need to provide a deed for any property you own free and clear. If you are still paying for the property, supply the name, address and account number for mortgage lenders. Know the current value of all real estate owned and the mortgage balances owed on the property.

7. If you are self-employed, have a financial statement that has been prepared by a disinterested third party and your past two years tax returns.

8. List automobiles you own by make and model, year and present value.

9. Estimate the replacement value of your furniture and personal property. This figure is usually in round numbers such as, $10,000, $15,000, $30,000, etc.

10. You may count alimony and child support, if you choose. If you do, you will probably be asked for a copy of your divorce decree and to verify receiving the monthly payments.

11. If you are vested in a retirement fund, determine the vested amount and add it to your assets. Vested means the amount you could have if you left your company.

LIABILITIES

1. List all debts. For credit cards, have card names, account numbers, present balances and minumum monthly payment. Try to have the most recent statements for all of your credit cards and bank accounts.

2. For all other debt, list who you pay, address, account number, *minimum* monthly payment and balance owing.

3. You will be required to list any alimony, child support or separate maintenance payments. If you make such payments, you will probably be asked to supply a copy of your divorce decree for verification.

SELF EMPLOYED

All self employed persons will be asked to provide income tax returns for the two most recent years. Corporate taxes will be required if your business is incorporated. The returns are needed to determine your present income and the strength of your business that provides your income.

You will also need an up to date profit and loss statement and, most likely an up to date financial statement. These will need to be prepared by a disinterested third party, in most cases.

If you hold a 25%, or larger, interest in any other business, tax returns and profit and loss statement will need to be provided.

VETERANS

Veterans will need to provide the DD Form 214. If this cannot be located, your mortgage lender and the Veterans Administration can help you.

SUMMARY

If you have all of the above listed information, your application will be off to a good start. Should you be unable to provide any necesary information at application, obtain it as quickly as possible and deliver it to the mortgage company. If you cannot provide some of the information, tell the loan officer, or processor, and they will help. Sometimes they may be able to give you ideas for obtaining the needed information.

The sooner your file is complete, the quicker your loan can be processed and approved.

CHAPTER SIX

Processing the Loan and Follow-Up

The job of processing your loan requires skill and diligence. The processor has to mail out verifications to your employer, your bank references and others, depending upon the information you supplied.

A credit report is ordered. Appraisal arranged and maybe a survey. Sometimes the survey is arranged by another agency.

The processor has to make sure all verifications received back are properly filled out and that other material requested and received contains the needed information. They also follow-up on any information that is not returned in a timely manner. Since there may be up to fifty loans being processed by your processor, their time is precious.

Processing is a tedious and exacting task. Depending on who the investor is for your loan, the investor guidelines have to be met exactly. If every applicant called their processor with frequent update questions, the processor's valuable time would be spent on the phone with loan applicants instead of processing loans.

Call your processor once or twice a week to see what has or has not been received. Ask if there is anything you can do to help. How can you help? Alert your employer or your company's personnel office that verification forms are being sent to them and ask them to complete and return the forms as soon as possible. Follow up with personnel, or with whoever receives the forms, to verify that the forms were received and returned. You might also check with your bank, former landlords and former, or present, mortgage companies to verify that they have received their forms. Ask them to fill them out and return them as soon as they can. Follow up on these also.

If problems develop between you and your processor, or if you feel you are not receiving good service, talk with your loan officer, the branch manager or the processing manager. Remember, try to remain calm at all times. Be courteous and friendly - though firm. A friendly, hard working processor is worth a fortune.

After completely processing your loan, it will be submitted to an underwriter for aproval. The underwriter makes sure the loan meets all of the necessary investor guidelines and approves, suspends or rejects the loan. A loan is suspended when something has been left out or there is an incompletion. Once the necessary information has been added, the underwriter will again examine the loan and approve or disapprove it. Once the loan has been approved, the loan is ready to have closing papers drawn.

CHAPTER SEVEN

Closing the Loan

Closing is normally a simple procedure for both buyer and seller. You show up, sign, sign and sign and either pay or receive money. Whether you close at a title company, mortgage company, bank or a realtor's office, you should have an experienced closer who will explain each of the many papers you will sign and guide you through the whole thing.

Just make sure the interest rate on your closing papers is the same rate you agreed to with the mortgage company. Then sign, sign and sign.

Your closer will have told you how much money to bring to your closing. During all of the signing, you will be asked to pay your down payment and closing costs.

After the closing is completed, your closer will call the mortgage lender and/or send the closing papers to the lender. The lender will confirm that the papers are correct then fund the loan by transferring the proper funds.

CHAPTER EIGHT

Ways to Save Money!!!

The basic charges for your loan are going to be similar at nearly all mortgage companies. You will pay about $50 to $75 for a credit report and from $150 to $200 for a survey. Some companies have an 'application fee' of $200, or more, and there will be an appraisal that will cost from $140 to $350, or more, depending on whether your loan is a VA, FHA or conventional. A VA and FHA appraisal is around $140 to $150 and conventional around $350. All of these charges are fairly standard. The Veterans Administration and FHA set the maximum appraisal costs for their loans. Ask the various mortgage companies the cost for appraisals and ask if they have any application, or other, fees.

Where you can save money is on the discount points and interest rate and by understanding the loan process. You save money on the interest rate by calling different mortgage companies and comparing rates, discount points and origination fees.

Discount points and the origination fee are normally paid from your cash resources at closing. The cost of the interest rate is paid monthly in your payment. If you want to save some of your cash, you might take a slightly higher interest rate with lower discount points. If, however, you want a slightly lower monthly payment and can afford to pay more at closing, you may want to get a slightly lower interest rate with slightly higher discount points.

Generally, for every 1/8% of interest rate reduction, expect to add one (1) discount point. For every 1/8% of increased interest, expect to reduce the discount points by about 1/2 point. Remember, each discount point equals

1% of the loan amount.

Mortgage companies operate in different ways when setting rates. Some companies call their branch offices daily and give rates, discount points and origination fees and the branches have to quote those rates exactly. Other companies call their branch offices with rates but the branch offices and loan personnel are allowed to quote higher rates and/or discount points. In the case of the latter, the rates called to the branches are basically the lowest rates the company wants to accept. If, for example, a loan officer is able to get an additional 1/8% interest rate, or additional discount points, then the extra amount is usually split 50-50 between the company and the loan officer. This is considered bonus or commission for the loan officer.

To guard against that, call several branches of the same company, during the same part of the day if possible, and compare their rates. If they are all the same, you can be fairly certain they are quoting the lowest rates possible for them. If some are different, ask them why and tell them their other branches are quoting lower rates for the same loan. Ask them for their lowest rate.

The offices that quote higher rates are not trying to cheat you. They are under an obligation to their company to make a profit. Buy quoting a higher rate, they take a chance of losing your business. Most will get in line with their other branches and give you the rate the others are quoting.

When you find a rate and company you like, make an appointment as soon as possible. Remember, the rates are subject to change daily. In very uncertain market conditions, the rates may change several times a day. If you make an appointment with a company that changes rates in the afternoon, be sure to check their rates early in the morning. You may want to go in early in order to get a rate you like rather than go in the afternoon and take a chance on the rate increasing. However, it could go down, too. Generally, the rates change in small steps. An interest rate may change 1/8% up or down and discount points may change 1/4 to 1/2 up or down.

If your rate has been floating while your loan is being processed, you will be notified when the loan has been approved. The person calling you will usually tell you what the current rate is and ask if that is all right with you. Before answering, call other branches of the same company. If there are no other branches locally, call other local mortgage lenders and see how their rates compare with the one your company quoted you. Also, ask the person who called you with loan approval if the interest rate they quoted is the current lowest rate available through that office. You can really assure yourself of saving money by doing this.

Buying a home is an emotional experience, especially when you are told you have been approved. Most people accept the interest rate quoted, when told of approval, and most of the time the rate is competitive with other local rates. It is, however, easy to add an extra 1/8% to the interest rate or an extra 1/4 to 1/2 to the discount points to add to a branch, or loan officer's, commission. Many companies do not allow that and few loan officers or processors will attempt it, but assure yourself by making several comparative phone calls. An extra 1/4 discount point, on a $90,000 loan, equals $225 ($90,000 x .0025). That makes the calls worth while and takes very little time.

Most mortgage companies quote and give competitive rates. I do not want to alarm you and make you think you are probably going to have to watch closely every move the mortgage company makes. That is not necessary. But, since most people are not familiar with how mortgage companies operate, you can use this information to assure yourself you are getting a good deal.

If you feel you have been unjustly or unfairly treated, ask to speak to supervisors until you reach one who can help you with your complaint. Remember, you are the customer and your business is important to the lending company.

CHAPTER NINE

Smile and Be Prepared

Remember, buying a home is an emotional experience. If you become frustrated during the process, talk to your realtor, loan officer or processor - and smile.

If you really encounter problems, and have a realtor helping you, your realtor can be a big help. The realtor has probably dealt with mortgage companies before and maybe has encountered the same problem. They will be anxious to see your loan approved, closed and funded because that is when they get paid.

By the same token, the loan officer and processor will usually receive commissions when the loan is completed. They, too, are anxious to successfully complete your loan. Talk with them about any concerns you have.

You always have the option of going to their boss, and as high as you want, to get answers to your concerns. You seldom have to do this but it is available to you.

If you feel you have been treated illegally, contact a local office of your state's Attorney General. Tell them what has happened and they will help you if they feel a complaint is justified. A letter from the Attorney General's office gets action. Even better, the cost is free. A private attorney will cost you money. Very few of you will ever have to take this step.

Again, try to smile your way through any problems and the problems will seem to be solved easier and with little effort.

AUTHOR'S COMMENTS

Thank you for purchasing this book. I would appreciate hearing from you. Your comments, suggestions and critiques are important to me. Should you have any questions, please write. I will, if at all possible, answer your letter.

If you are not pleased with this book and feel it has not been useful to you, I will refund your purchase price for six months from the date of purchase, with a smile.

Good luck to you and I earnestly hope all of you get your dream house.

GLOSSARY

MORTGAGE LOAN LANGUAGE

-A-

Acceleration Clause — A common provision of a mortgage and note providing that the entire principal shall become immediately due and payable in the event of default, transfer of title, etc.

Acquisition Cost — In a HUD-FHA transaction, the sum of the price paid for the property and any costs of closing, repairs, or financing (except discounts in other than a refinance transaction) properly paid by the borrower. Does not include prepaid discounts in a purchase transaction, mortgage insurance premiums, etc.

Adjustable Rate Mortgage (ARM) — A mortgage loan with provisions for periodic increases or decreases in interest rates as a specified index changes over the life of the loan. Most common ARM types are the 1, 3, or 5 year ARMs based respectively on the yield movements of the 1-year T-Bill, the 3 and 5-year T-Note indexes. Opposite of a fixed rate mortgage.

Adjustment Cap — Generally associated with ARM loans. The maximum the interest rate on a mortgage loan can increase or decrease per adjustment. A 2% adjustment cap means that the interest rate will not increase or decrease more than 2% at the next adjustment.

Amortization — Gradual debt reduction. Normally, the reduction is made according to a pre-determined schedule for installment payments. HUD-FHA and VA regulations require that insured or guaranteed mortgages provide for amortization in equal monthly payments over the term of the loan, except that the payments in the early years of a Graduated Payment Mortgage may change from year to year, and those of an Adjustable Rate Mortgage may change from time to time, subject to certain restrictions.

Annual Percentage Rate (APR) — The cost of credit in relation to the amount financed. The lender is required to state the APR on loan documents.

Appraisal — An estimate of value of a piece of real estate by an appraiser who is considered to be an expert in real estate property valuations.

Appreciation — Any increase in value. The opposite of depreciation.

APR — See 'Annual Percentage Rate'

ARM — 'Adjustable Rate Mortgage'

Arm's Length Transaction — A transaction between a willing buyer and a willing seller with no undue influence imposed on either party and where there is no relationship between the parties except that of the specified transaction.

Assumption — The act of taking over a mortgage obligation incurred by the original borrower. The new buyer assumes the mortgage and assumes title to the property.

-B-

Balance Sheet — A statement of financial condition of a business organization showing assets, liabilities, capital and including net worth as of a given date.

Balloon Loan — A mortgage with periodic installments of principal and interest that do not fully amortize the loan. The balance of the mortgage is due in a lump sum at a specified date in the future, usually at the end of the term.

Basis Point — 1/100th of 1%. 50 basis points equals .50%, or 1/2 of 1%. Used to describe the amount of change in yield in many debt instruments, including mortgages.

Borrower — A mortgagor who receives funds in the form of a loan with the obligation of repaying the loan in full, with interest, if applicable.

Bridge Loan — A temporary mortgage or note to help a homebuyer obtain funds to purchase another home prior to the sale of a currently owned home.

Buydown — The initial cash paid, generally in the form of discount points, to reduce the borrower's payment. See 'Temporary Buydown and Permanent Buydown'.

-C-

Cap — See 'Adjustment Cap'.

Cash Flow — The spendable cash (income) from an income-producing property after deducting from gross income all operating expenses and debt service.

Ceiling — The maximum interest rate that can be charged on an ARM loan according to the Cap provisions of the loan.

Certificate of Eligibility — Evidence that the veteran is elegible for VA Loan guaranty benefits. The face of the form identifies the veteran. The reverse provides details on the status and extent of the veteran's eligibility.

Certificate of Reasonable Value (CRV) — A document issued by the VA establishing a maximum value and loan amount for a mortgage to be guaranteed by VA.

Certificate of Title — A written statement furnished by an abstract of title company, or attorney, to a client, stating that the title to a piece of property is legally vested in the present owner.

Certificate of Veteran's Status — The document given to veterans or reservists who have served 90 days of continuous active duty (including training time). This document enables veterans to obtain lower down payments on certain FHA insured loans.

Chattel — Personal property.

Closing — The conclusion of a transaction. In real estate, closing includes the delivery of a deed, financial adjustments, the signing of notes and the disbursment of funds necessary to the sale or loan transaction.

Closing Costs — Money paid by any party to the transaction to effect the closing of a mortgage loan. Does not include prepaid expenses, apportionments, and the like, but does normally include an origination fee, title insurance, survey, attorney's fees, etc. In HUD-FHA transactions, all closing costs are added to the appraised value of the property to establish the 'FHA Value' on which the maximum insurable mortgage is based. Closing costs paid by the borrower are added to the sales price to establish 'Acquisition Cost'.

Co-Mortgagor — A second borrower, not the spouse of the principal borrower, who assumes equal responsibility for the debt and a share of ownership of the property. Income and obligations of the co-mortgagor are considered in the underwriting process as though he or she were the principal mortgagor.

Comparables — An abbreviation for 'comparable properties' used for comparative purposes in the appraisal process. Facilities of reasonably the same size and location with similar amenities. Properties that have been sold recently and have characteristics similar to the property under consideration, thereby indicating the approximate fair market value of the subject property.

Conforming — Refers to conforming loan limits, normally set by FNMA/FHLMC. Non-Conforming, or loan amounts over this limit, usually handled by secondary market lenders.

Condominimum — A form of ownership of real property. The purchaser receives title to a particular unit and an undivided, or proportionate, interest in cetain common areas. A condominium generally defines each unit as a separately owned space to the interior surfaces of the perimeter walls, floors and ceilings. Title to the common areas is in terms of percentages and refers to the entire project, less the separately owned units.

Conventional Loan — A mortgage loan made by an institutonal lender without FHA insurance or a VA guarantee.

Convey — The act of transferring title to real property from one party to another.

Conveyance — The document, such as a deed, lease, or mortgage, used to effect a transfer.

Credit Report — A report to a prospective lender on the credit standing of a prospective borrower. Used to help determine credit worthiness.

CRV — See 'Certificate of Reasonable Value'.

-D-

Debt Service — The periodic payment of principal and interest on mortgage loans.

Deed — A document by which the ownership of land is transferred from one party to another.

Deed of Trust — In some states, the document used in place of a mortgage. A type of security instrument conveying title in trust to a third party covering a particular piece of property. It is used to secure the payment of a note. A conveyance of the title to land to a trustee as collateral security for the payment of a debt with the condition that the trustee will reconvey the title on payment of the debt, with the power of the trustee to sell the property and pay the debt, in the event of a default on the part of the debtor.

Department of Housing and Urban Development — Established by the Housing and Urban Development Act of 1965 to supersede the Housing and Home Finance Agency and give administration of the nation's housing and urban development programs Cabinet status. It is responsible for the implementation and administration of government housing and urban development programs. The broad range of programs includes community planning and development, low-rent public housing, mortgage insurance for residential mortgages (FHA), equal opportunity in housing, research and technology.

Deposit — 1) A sum of money given to bind a sale of real estate.
2) A sum of money give to assure payment, or an advance of funds, in the processing of a loan. Also known as 'Earnest Money'.

Depreciation — The decline in value of an asset due to its wear and tear from use and the passage of time. This amount is a non-cash expense to the company that reduces the company's tax liability. It also reduces the value of the company's assets, at least on paper.

Real Property Depreciation — Decline in value of real property such as a building, factory, or warehouse. This does not include land, since land is not permitted to be depreciated.

Chattel Depreciation — Decline in value of a company's property such as desks, trucks, office equipment, etc. Personal property is property that can be moved, whereas real property is affixed and, under normal conditions, cannot be moved.

Discount Point — Points are a device used to equalize interest rate yeilds. One point is one percent of the loan amount. Each discount point increases the interest yield (on 30 year fixed rate mortgages) one eighth.

Draw — Disbursement of a portion of the loan proceeds, usually at a predetermined point in the construction, or rehabilitation, schedule, to pay for work already completed. The balance of the proceeds is retained until the next scheduled draw, or until completion of the construction or rehabilitation work, to protect the lender against the contractor's failure to complete the work as scheduled.

Due on Sale Clause — A special type of acceleration clause that demands payment of the entire loan balance upon sale, or other transfer of the title.

Duplex — Two separate living units within the same building.

-E-

Easement — A right to use the land of another for a specific purpose, such as a right of way; or for utilities (an incorporeal interest in land). An easement appurtenant passes with the land when conveyed.

Effective Gross Income (Personal) — Normal annual income including overtime, before deductions, that is regular or guaranteed. It may be from more than one source. Salary is generally the principal source but other income may be significant and stable, and thus qualify. Effective Gross Income is used as the basis for borrower qualification by most conventional lenders and private mortgage insurers. Contrast with 'Net Effective Income'.

Encumberance — Any lien, such as a mortgage, tax lien, or judgement lien; also an easement, a restriction on the use of the land, or an outstanding dower right that may diminish the value of the property.

Entitlement — The VA home loan benefit used to guarantee a VA home loan. Also called Guaranty.

Escalation — Increasing the interest rate. Normally occurs when a loan is transferred or assumed and the original interest rate is increased to current market rates.

Escrow — Funds which are set aside and held in trust, usually for payment of taxes and insurance on real property. Also earnest deposits held pending loan closing.

Execute — To complete, finish, or in real estate deeds, to sign, seal and deliver.

-F-

Fannie Mae — See 'Federal National Mortgage Association'.

Farmers Home Administration (FmHA) — A government agency within the Department of Agriculture that operates under the Consolidated Farm and Rural Development Act of 1921 and Title V of the Housing Act of 1949. This agency provides financing to farmers and other qualified borrowers in communities of less than 25,000 who are unable to obtain loans elsewhere. The agency makes loans with funds borrowed from the U.S. Treasury.

Federal Home Loan Bank Board (FHLBB) — A regulatory and supervisory agency for federally chartered savings institutions. It oversees the operations of the Federal Savings and Loan Insurance Corporation (FSLIC) and the Federal Home Loan Mortgage Corporation (FHLMC).

Federal Home Loan Mortgage Corporation (FHLMC - 'Freddie Mac') — A private corporation authorized by congress. It sells participation sales certificates secured by pools of conventional mortgage loans, their principal and interest guaranteed by the Federal government through the FHLMC. It also sells Government National Mortgage

Association bonds to raise funds to finance the purchase of mortgages.

Federal Housing Administration (FHA) — Formerly an independent agency, now a part of the Department of Housing and Urban Development (HUD), without a separate organizational identity and sometimes referred to as 'HUD' or 'HUD-FHA'. Its main activity is the insurance of residential mortgage loans, home improvement loans and land development loans made by private lenders. It sets standards for construction and the mortgage lending industry that, while they are mandatory only with respect to loans insured by HUD-FHA, have generally become accepted as industry-wide standards. HUD-FHA does not lend money, nor does it plan, or construct, housing.

Federal National Mortgage Association (FNMA - 'Fannie Mae') — Formerly a government agency within the Housing and Home Finance Agency, it was made a private corporation when the Government GNMA assumed the government-supported functions of the former FNMA and FNMA became a private corporation, created by congress to support the secondary mortgage market. It purchases and sells residential mortgages insured by FHA, or guaranteed by VA, as well as conventional mortgages.

Federal Truth-in-Lending Disclosure Statement — A form designed and reproduced locally by lenders to comply with disclosure requirements of the Federal Truth-in-Lending Act.

Fee Simple — The greatest possible interest a person can have in real estate.

FHA — See 'Federal Housing Administration'.

FHA Case Number — The number used to identify a HUD-FHA mortgage in HUD's records.

FHA Value — The value established by FHA as the basis for determining the maximum mortgage that may be insured on a specific property. It includes the appraised value of the property and the HUD-FHA estimate of required closing costs.

First Mortgage — A real estate loan that creates a primary lien against real property.

First Time Home Buyer — In most government programs, a person applying for mortgage insurance, or guaranty, who has not owned real estate during the three years immediately preceding the date of the application. There are some exceptions. For example, a person who sold a home to move to a distant community might qualify as a first-time home buyer in the new community.

Fixed Rate Mortgage — A loan whose interest rate does not change during the life of the loan. The opposite of an Adjustable Rate Mortgage.

FNMA — See 'Federal National Mortgage Association'.

Foreclosure — A court action initiated by the mortgagee, or a lienor, for the purpose of having the court order that the debtor's real estate be sold to pay the mortgage, or other lien (Mechanic's-lien or judgement).

Fourplex — Four separate living units within the same building.

-G-

Gift Affidavit — An unnumbered, locally produced form, standardized locally by most HUD-FHA and VA offices. When an applicant intends to rely upon a gift to meet settlement requirements, both HUD-FHA and VA require evidence that the funds are truly a gift, from someone who would logically be expected to make the gift, and that repayment is neither required nor expected. Some offices also require verification that the doner actually has the funds on deposit.

Ginnie Mae — See 'Government National Mortgage Association'.

GNMA — See 'Government National Mortgage Association'.

Government National Mortgage Association (GNMA - 'Ginnie Mae') — On September 1, 1968, Congress enacted legislation to partition FNMA into two continuing corporate entities. GNMA assumed responsibility for the special assistance loan program and the management and liquidation functions of the older FNMA. Also, GNMA administers the mortgage backed securities program that channels new sources for funds into residential financing through the sale of privately issued securities guaranteed by GNMA.

Graduated Payment Loan — Usually a deferred interest mortgage whereby the monthly payments start out low and gradually increase over a specified period of time, generally 5 or 10 years. Also, Graduated Payment Mortgage.

Gross Income — See 'Effective Gross Income'.

Guarantee Period — The length of time a mortgage rate and/or points will be guaranteed. Usually 45 or 60 days.

Guaranteed Loan — A loan guaranteed by VA, FmHA, or any other interested party.

-H-

Hazard Insurance — A contract whereby an insurer, for a premium, undertakes to compensate the insured for loss on a specific property due to certain hazards such as fire, wind, theft, vandalism, etc.

Home Loan — A mortgage loan secured by a residence for one, two, three, or four families. Also known as a 'single-family mortgage', even though the property may be designed for more than one family.

Home Owners Association — An organization of homeowners residing within a particular development, whose major purpose is to maintain and provide community faciliies and services for the common enjoyment of the residents.

Homeowners Policy — A multiple peril hazard insurance policy commonly called a 'package policy'. It is available to owners of a private dwelling and covers the dwelling and contents in the case of loss due to specific hazards enumerated in the policy. It generally also provides insurance against loss due to personal liability related to the property.

Homestead Estate — In some states, the home and property occupied by an owner are protected by law (usually up to a certain amount), from attachment and sale, for the claims

54

of creditors. There may also be specific exemptions from taxation and other benefits.

Housing and Urban Development, Department of — See 'Department of Housing and Urban Development'.

HUD — See 'Department of Housing and Urban Development'.

HUD-1 — See 'Settlement Statement'.

-I-

Improved Land — Land having utilities, roads, or other improvements.

Improvements — Those additions to raw land that normally increase its value, such as buildings, streets and sewers.

Income and Expense Statement (Related to Rental Properties) — An unnumbered form, produced locally by many HUD-FHA offices and used to provide details permitting an analysis of the net income available to an applicant from rental properties other than the subject property. Even where a prescribed format for providing this information does not exist, it must be provided with the application.

Index — A reference point. For instance, the 1 year T (Treasury) - Bill is often designated in the index on 1-year ARM loan programs. At the first adjustment, the new interest rate will be the current T-Bill rate plus the gross margin stated in the note. If the index decreased 1%, then the borrower's rate would drcrease 1%.

Index Movement — The fluctuations of a particular index rate over a period of time.

Index Value — The stated yield of an index stated as a percentage.

Indirect Costs — Costs in erecting a new building, not involved with either site preparation or building construction; for example, a building permit, land survey, overhead expenses such as insurance and payroll taxes and builder's profit.

Installments — The regular, periodic payment that a borrower agrees to make to a mortgagee.

Installment Contract — A contract for the sale of real estate wherein purchase price is paid in installments over an extended period of time, by the purchaser, who is in possession, with the title retained by the seller until the final payment is made. The purchaser's payments are forfeited upon default.

Installment Note — A note requiring periodic payment of a specified sum to satisfy a debt.

Institutional Lender — A financial institution that invests in mortgages and carries them in its own portfolio. Mutual savings banks, life insurance companies, commercial banks, pension and trust funds and savings and loan associations are examples.

Insurance — A contract for indemnification (compensate) against loss.

Interest — Consideration, in the form of money, paid for the use of money, usually expressed as an annual percentage. Also, a right, share, or title in property.

Interim Finanacing — A temporary construction loan made during the completion of a building or a home, usually replaced by a permanent loan after completion and/or sale.

Investor — The holder of a mortgage, or the permanent lender, for whom the mortgage banker services the loan. Any person, or institution, that invests in mortgages.

-J-

Jumbo Loan — A loan that exceeds the dollar amount of conforming loans.

-L-

Landlord — Owner or lessor of real property.

Late Charge — An additional charge a borrower is required to pay as a penalty for failure to pay a regular installment when due.

Lease — A written document containing the conditions under which the possession and use of a real and/or personal property are given, by the owner, to another for a stated period and for a stated consideration.

Legal Description — A property description recognized by law, which is sufficient to locate and identify the property without oral testimony.

Lessee — One holding rights of possession and use of property under a lease.

Lessor — One who owns property and leases it to a lessee.

Level Payment Mortgage — A mortgage that provides for a constant, fixed payment at periodic intervals during its term. Part of each payment is credited to interest, with the balance of the payment used to reduce the principal.

Lien — A legal hold or claim of one person, on the property of another, as security for a debt or charge. The right given by law to satisfy a debt.

Life of Loan — Contract term, in years, of a mortgage.

Lifetime Cap — Generally associated with ARM loans. Limits the maximum interest rate over the life of a loan.

Liquidity — The ability of an individual or business to quickly convert assets into cash, without incurring a considerable loss.

Limited Partnership — A partnership that consists of one or more general partners who are fully liable and one or more limited partners who are liable only for the amount of their investment.

Listing — A written authorization to sell or lease real estate.

Loan Closing — See 'Closing'.

Loan Submission — A package of pertinent papers and documents regarding specific property or properties. It is delivered to a prospective lender for review and consideration for the purpose of making a mortgage loan.

Loan-to-Value Ratio (LTVR) —
1) The relationship between the amount of the mortgage loan and the appraised value of the security, expressed

as a percentage of the appraised value.

2) In HUD-FHA transactions, the relationship between the amount of the mortgage loan and the 'FHA Value', which is the sum of the appraised value of the property and the estimated closing costs.

Loan Verification — An unnumbered, locally produced form, used to request verifications of obligations where the creditor refuses to provide information to credit bureaus and is not identified by the applicant as a depository holding funds of the applicant.

-M-

MAI (Member Appraisal Institute) — The highest professional designation awarded by the American Institute of Real Estate Appraisers.

Margin — Normally associated with ARM loans. The amount added to the index to achieve the net (net margin), or gross (gross margin) yield at adjustment.

Market Value — Most probable price, in terms of money, which a property should bring in a competitive and open market under all conditions requiste to a fair sale, the buyer and seller each acting prudently, knowledgably, and assuming the price is not affected by undue stimulus. The value of a property determined by comparable sales, the actual sales price or the capitalization method.

Mechanic's Lien — A lien placed on a property as security for payment for work performed in the construction or rehabilitation of a property, or for materials used or furnished for construction.

MI — See 'Mortgage Insurance'.

MIL — See 'Mortgage Information Letter'.

MIP — See 'Mortgage Insurance Premium'.

Mortgage — A conveyance of an interest in real property given as security for the payment of a debt. In its simplest form, a mortgage permits foreclosure if the debt is not paid, but the foreclosure is usually a judicial proceeding, in court. After foreclosure, the property is sold, usually by an officer of the court, to satisfy the debt.

Mortgage Amortization Schedule — See 'Amortization'.

Mortgage-backed Securities — Bond-type investment securities representing an undivided interest in a pool of mortgages or trust deeds. Income from the underlying mortgages is used to pay off the securities.

Mortgage Banker — A firm, or individual, active in the field of mortgage banking. Mortgage bankers, as local representatives of regional, or national, institutional lenders, act as correspondents between lenders and borrowers. More and more frequently, though, mortgage bankers are, themselves, becoming institutional lenders, holding mortgages in their own portfolios, as the basis for mortgage-backed securities that they issue.

Mortgage Banking — The packaging of mortgage loans, secured by real property, to be sold to a permanent investor, with servicing retained for the life of the loan, for a fee. The origination, sale and servicing of loans by a firm or individual. The investor-correspondent system is the foundation of the mortgage banking industry.

Mortgage Broker — A firm, or individual, who brings the borrower and lender together, receiving a commission if a sale is the resulting product. A mortgage broker does not retain servicing.

Mortgage Information Letter A letter issued by the mortgagee, or title company which indicates the payoff balance of a loan, or any other requirements, to pay off, or make, a loan on real property.

Mortgage Insurance — Insurance that protects the lender by lowering their risk exposure on conventional loans. Normally required on loans above an 80% loan-to-value-ratio. Protects the lender against borrower default and property value declines.

Mortgage Insurance Premium (MIP) — Insurance paid on FHA loans at 1/2 percent per year, paid each month as part of the regular payment. It is insurance from FHA that insures the lender against loss due to a borrower's default.

Mortgagee — The lender of money for property. One who holds a mortgage on property, as security on a loan.

Mortgagee Clause — A special clause that may be attached to a hazard insurance policy covering mortgaged real property.

Mortgagor — One who borrows money, giving a mortgage, or deed of trust on real property as security.

-N-

Narative Appraisal Report — A detailed written presentation of the facts and reasoning behind an appraiser's estimate of value.

Negative Amortization — The opposite of amortization. Can occur when the actual payment rate is less than the required interest rate, resulting in an increase in the principal balance, usually due to deferred interest. The deferred interest added to the loan balance creates negative amortization. Can occure in ARM loans with payment caps.

Net Effective Income — Gross income with taxes, social security and monthly bills deducted.

Net Worth — The value of all assets, including cash, less total liabilities. It is often used as an underwriting guideline to indicate credit worthiness and financial strength.

Non-Conforming — Loans over conforming limits. Loans over conforming limits are usually handled by private market investors. Same as 'Jumbo loans'.

Note Rate — The interest rate stated in the note.

-O-

Origination Fee — A fee or charge for the work involved in the evaluation, preparation and submission of a proposed mortgage loan. Often improperly considered a part of the discount. It usually helps to offset the lender's overhead in making a loan. Generally quoted in points.

Originator — A person who solicits builders, brokers and others, to obtain applications for mortgage loans. Origination is the process by which the mortgage banker brings into being a mortgage secured by real property. May also be called a loan officer.

-P-

Permanent Buydown — Reduces the interest rate and monthly payments over the full amortization period of a loan.

Permanent Loan — A long term loan, or mortgage, that is fully amortized and extended for a period not less than ten years.

PMI — Stands for 'Private Mortgage Insurance'.

PITI — Stands for Principal, Interest, Taxes and Insurance. The principal and interest payment on most loans is fixed for the term of the loan. The taxes and insurance payments may be adjusted to reflect changes in taxes and insurance costs.

Plans and Specifications — Architectural and engineering drawings and specifications for construction of a building or project. They include a description of materials to be used and the manner in which they are to be applied.

Plat — A map representing a piece of land subdivided into lots with streets, boundaries, easements and dimensions shown thereon. It is usually recorded and made a part of the public record.

Points — One point is equal to one percent of the principal loan amount. Loan discount points are a one-time charge assessed at closing, by the lender, to increase the yield on the mortgage loan to a competitive position with other types of investments.

Prepayment Penalty — A consideration (usually money) paid to the lender or investor, when a borrower pays off a loan prior to maturity. Not a part of all loans.

Prepayment Privilege — The right given a borrower to pay all, or part, of a debt before its maturity.

Principal Loan Balance — The outstanding amount of the mortgage debt, exclusive of interest and other charges. Same as the loan amount.

Private Mortgage Insurance (PMI) — Insurance written by a private company, protecting the mortgage lender against loss occasioned by a mortgage default.

Processing — The preparation of a mortgage loan application and supporting documents for consideration by a lender or insurer.

Pro-Rate — To allocate proportionate shares of income (such as rents), or of an obligation (such as taxes and insurance premiums), paid or due, between seller and buyer, at closing.

-Q-

Quitclaim Deed — A deed that transfers only such interest, title, or right a grantor may have, at the time the conveyance is executed.

-R-

Real Estate — See 'Real Property'.

Real Property — Land and appurtenances, including anything of a permanent nature, such as structures, trees, minerals and the interest, benefits and inherent rights thereof.

Realtor — A real estate broker, or an associate, holding active membership in the local real estate board affiliated with the National Association of Realtors.

Redlining — The alleged identification, by some lenders and/or investors, of specific geographic areas, for the purpose of denying real estate loans or varying lending terms in a discriminatory pattern.

Refinancing — The repayment of a debt from the proceeds of a new loan using the same property as security.

Remaining Economic Life — The number of years of useful life left to a building from the date of appraisal.

Release of Liability — An agreement by a lender to terminate the personal obligation of a mortgagor in connection with the payment of a debt, usually when another mortgagor has agreed to assume the liability. HUD-FHA and VA reserve the right to approve such releases in advance, when the mortgage is insured or guaranteed by them.

Rent — Consideration paid for use, or occupancy, of property, buildings or dwelling units.

RESPA — Real Estate Settlement Procedures Act. A Federal law that requires lenders to provide home mortgage borrowers, in advance, with information of known, or estimated, settlement costs. RESPA also limits the amount lenders may require to be held in escrow for real estate taxes and insurance, requires the disclosure of known settlement costs to both buyers and sellers by the person conducting the settlement and outlaws certain referral fees.

-S-

Sales Contract — A deliberate, written agreement between competent parties stating terms and conditions of a sale.

Second Mortgage — A mortgage recorded subsequent to another mortgage and subordinate to the first one. Second lien.

Secondary Mortgage Market — The place where primary mortgage lenders sell the mortgages they make to obtain more funds to originate more loans, providing liquidity for primary lenders.

Security — The collateral given, deposited, or pledged, to secure the fulfillment of an obligation or the payment of a debt.

Servicing — The duties of the mortgage banker as a loan correspondent as specified in the servicing agreement, for which a fee is received. The collection for an investor of payments, interest, principal and trust items, such as hazard insurance and taxes, on a note, by the borrower, in accordance with terms of the note. Servicing also includes operational procedures covering accounting, bookkeeping, insurance administration, tax records, loan payment follow-up, delinquent loan follow-up and loan analysis.

Settlement Statement — HUD Form 1. A statement showing full details of the loan closing, including costs paid by both the buyer and the seller and a detailed breakdown of the manner in which the loan proceeds were distributed. The Real Estate Settlement Procedures Act (RESPA) requires that this standardized form be used in all loan closings in which the Federal Government is involved in any way, even though the loan itself may not be insured or guaranteed by a government agency. For practical purposes, the form must be used with all mortgage loan closings.

Simple Interest — Interest which is computed only on the principal balance.

SRA — Senior Residential Appraiser, Society of Real Estate Appraisers.

SREA — Society of Real Estate Appraisers. The Society awards the following professional designations: Senior Residential Appraiser (SRA); Senior Real Property Appraiser (SRPA); and Senior Real Estate Analyst (SREA).

Survey — A measurement of land, prepared by a registered land surveyor, showing the location of the land, with reference to known points, its dimensions and the location and dimensions of any improvements.

Sweat Equity — Equity created by a purchaser performing work on property being purchased. It directly increases the value of the property.

-T-

Take Out Commitment — A lender agrees to issue a permanent loan commitment to replace temporary financing, usually to replace a construction loan.

Tax Lien — A claim against property for the amount of its due and unpaid taxes.

Temporary Buydown — Lowers the borrowers payment for shorter periods than a permanent buydown. Any buydown that remains in effect for less than the full amortization period of a loan, is considered a temporary buydown. The most common type of buydown is a builder/seller subsidy.

Tenant — One who is not the owner but occupies real property with the consent of the owner and, in subordination to, the owner's title. The tenant is entitled to exclusive possession, use and enjoyment of the property, usually for a rent specified in a lease.

Title — The evidence of the right to, or ownership in, property. In the case of real estate, the documentary evidence of ownership is the title deed that specifies in whom the legal estate is vested and the history of ownership and transfers. Title may be acquired through purchase, inheritance, devise, gift, or through foreclosure of a mortgage.

Title Insurance — Insurance issued to owners of real property to protect them against arising by reason of defects in the title to real estate owned.

Townhouse — A residential unit on a small lot that has coincidential exterior limits with other similar units. Title to the unit and its lot is vested in the individual buyer, with a fractional interest in common areas, if any. Sometimes called 'Row House'.

Treasury Security — A security, such as T-Bills, Notes and Bonds, issued by the U.S. Treasury, to finance the national debt and government.

-U-

Underwriting — The analysis of risk and the matching of it to an appropriate rate and term.

Unencumbered Property — Property that is free and clear of debt.

Usury — Charging more for the use of money than allowed by law.

Usury Ceiling — A maximum legal rate, established by state law, for interest, discounts, or other fees that may be charged for nature, or type, of the loan.

-V-

VA — See 'Veterans Administration'.

Vacancy Factor — A percentage rate expressing the loss from gross rental income due to vacancy and collection losses.

Verification of Deposit — An unnumbered, locally produced form, to verify balances of accounts in banks, or other depositories, as stated on the mortgage application.

Verification of Employment — An unnumbered, locally produced form, used to send to previous and present employers for verification of previous and present employment, as stated on the mortgage application.

-W-

Warehousing — The borrowing of funds, by a mortgage banker, on a short-term basis, at a commercial bank, using permanent mortgage loans as collateral. This form of interim financing is used until the mortgages are sold to a permanent investor.

Wrap-Around Mortgage — A mortgage securing a debt that includes the balance due on an existing senior mortgage and an additional amount advanced by the wrap-around mortgagee. The new, larger loan usually allows a buyer to obtain a lower overall interest rate.